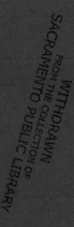

UFOs

Elaine Landau

The Millbrook Press ❑ *Brookfield, Connecticut*
Mysteries of Science

Photographs courtesy of Science Photo Library/Photo Researchers: pp. 8 (Julian Baum), 11 (David Hardy), 20 (David Parker), 34 (SETI Institute), 36 (John Mead); UPI/Bettmann: pp. 13, 27, 37, 38; Scala/Art Resource, NY: p. 15; AP/Wide World: pp. 18, 23, 29, 31.

Library of Congress Cataloging-in-Publication Data
Landau, Elaine.
UFOs / Elaine Landau.
p.   cm.
Includes bibliographical references and index.
Summary: Examines the possibility of sightings of unidentified flying objects and encounters with extraterrestrials, considering the reliability of eyewitness accounts and alternative explanations.
ISBN 1-56294-542-4 (lib. bdg.)
1. Unidentified flying objects—Juvenile literature.
[1. Unidentified flying objects.]   I. Title.
TL789.2.L315   1996
001.9'42—dc20   95-19733   CIP   AC

Published by The Millbrook Press, Inc.
2 Old New Milford Road, Brookfield, Connecticut 06804

For Illana Harkavi

Contents

UFO. . . UFO. . . Downed in New Mexico?

The excitement began in June 1947, when Kenneth Arnold, an experienced pilot flying his private plane, approached Mount Rainier, Washington. Suddenly, a brilliant flash of light appeared. Arnold hadn't seen where it came from before the light flashed again. Then the pilot spotted nine disk-shaped craft traveling at an estimated speed of more than 1,000 miles (1,610 kilometers) per hour.

Not certain what he had seen, Arnold reported the incident to the manager of the airport where he landed. News of the flashing disks quickly spread, and when Arnold arrived at his next destination, he was greeted by reporters anxious to know more. Once Arnold told them that the disks flew the way "a saucer would if you skipped it across the water," a reporter described the mysterious craft as "flying saucers."[1]

During the next two weeks, hundreds of similar sightings were reported. Some people who claim to have seen the "saucers" were respected community members, including airline pilots, teachers, law enforcement officers, and high-level military personnel.

By the first week of July, there had also been scattered reports that some of the saucer-shaped disks crashed. One especially noteworthy incident took place on the property of Mac Brazel, a New Mexico rancher. On June 14, 1947, Brazel was out inspecting his livestock with his neighbor's seven-year-old son, Timmy Proctor, when they came upon a mass of debris scattered across the land. The rancher realized it was like nothing he had ever seen before. The metal pieces were thin and light enough to blow in the breeze. Yet this surprisingly sturdy material could not be cut with a knife or burned with a match.

Mac Brazel knew he had stumbled on something strange. On July 6, he brought samples of the fallen debris to the sheriff's office in the town of Roswell, New Mexico, some 75 miles (about 121 kilometers) from the ranch. Sheriff George A. Wilcox thought it best to report the incident to the nearest military base. Shortly after he placed the call, several military officers arrived to learn more about what had occurred. After visiting the site, the military examiners believed they had found the remains of an extraterrestrial craft. And soon afterward, army public information officer Lieutenant Walter Haut issued a press release to that effect.

Even the military officers who came to Mac Brazel's
field to investigate what came to be known as
the Roswell Incident believed they had found the
remains of an extraterrestrial craft.

The incident quickly captured the media's attention, and the phones at the air base began ringing constantly. As it turned out, however, the unusual metallic debris might have been just the start of a still more unsettling discovery. It was rumored that military planes, scanning the area to make certain nothing was overlooked in the cleanup, spied a second crash site only miles from the first wreckage. But this time instead of merely finding portions of a downed spacecraft, people claimed that they also came across several nonhuman corpses.

Shortly afterward, what many believe to be a government cover-up began. Military officials of the Eighth Air Force issued a new statement declaring that what was first thought to have been the remains of an extraterrestrial craft was actually just a fallen weather balloon.

UFO buffs insist that, upon close scrutiny, the government's story does not hold up. Since the time of the crash a number of people either directly or indirectly involved have spoken out. Former Roswell mortician Glen Dennis reported that after the crash the air base's mortuary officer called to inquire if he had some 3½- or 4-foot (about 1-

Air Force officials at Fort Worth, Texas, examine the remains of the object found by Mac Brazel. Do they truly believe it is a downed weather balloon?

meter) -long baby coffins that were hermetically sealed (incapable of being penetrated by liquid or gas).

The evidence of the craft's destruction and of the recovery of alien corpses was further confirmed by a nurse at the army base hospital. She described the extraterrestrials as smaller than the average adult human as well as slimmer and more fragile-looking. The nurse noticed that the aliens' hands were different as well. She said they had only four fingers and the two middle ones were longer than the others.

Those who doubt that an alien craft crashed in New Mexico offer a very different explanation of what occurred. Their theory is based on a September 1994 Air Force document detailing Project Mogul, a once-secret government espionage (spying) program in which air balloons were sent into the upper atmosphere to detect vibrations from nuclear test blasts across the globe. Effectively monitoring distant nuclear blasts was deemed crucial to United States security, as it would alert the government if other countries were developing potentially devastating bombs.

After reviewing the Air Force report and interviews with both former Mogul officials and experts on the history of atomic spying, some individuals have concluded that the Roswell debris was actually downed Project Mogul equipment. Those who doubt the extraterrestrial story also think that claims of the U.S. government possessing alien corpses were overblown.

UFO sightings are not just a phenomenon
of the twentieth century. Look closely at the
upper right-hand corner of this painting,
which was done in the fifteenth century.

Despite the new evidence, many people persist in believing that an alien craft crashed at Roswell, New Mexico. Colonel Albert C. Trakowski, the retired Air Force officer who ran Project Mogul, explained their reluctance to believe the incident wasn't real: "This won't lay to rest. The psychology is simple: People believe what they want to believe. In New Mexico, flying-saucerism has become a minor industry. There are whole museums dedicated to the presentation of outrageous fictions."[2]

Sighting: Here, There, Everywhere

Some UFO enthusiasts feel that the Roswell incident was a minor part of a much larger UFO government cover-up. From the late 1940s to 1969, Project Blue Book served as the Air Force's UFO investigatory agency. Before its shutdown, the project submitted a 1,465-page report indicating "nothing has come from the study of UFOs."[1]

While Project Blue Book's findings were unimpressive, some people believe the agency itself was little more than a military public relations effort. For evidence, they point to a recovered government memo written on October 20, 1969, by Brigadier General C. H. Bolender indicating "reports of unidentified flying objects which could affect national security are not part of the Blue Book system."[2]

These individuals believe that the hunt for extraterrestrials has long been actively pursued by top military officials who have kept their findings secret in classified documents.

Yet despite government secrecy, UFO believers have still obtained a good deal of information on their own. In an important exchange of knowledge, civilians in various countries have begun to share information on extraterrestrial encounters.

One sighting of international interest took place in Israel in January 1992. There, a number of individuals reported seeing a spherelike object leave a fiery trail behind it in the night sky. The sphere flew north of the Sea of Galilee, then over Nazareth, and then went as far south as the Dead Sea. After an Israeli radio station reported the sightings, the station was swamped with calls from listeners claiming to have seen the sphere.

Another mysterious phenomenon, which some attribute to visitors from outer space, has occurred over a large portion of southern England every summer since 1976. Dur-

Although the government does not acknowledge UFO sightings, this photo, taken at Santa Ana, California, was part of a study done at the University of Colorado that was funded by the Air Force.

ing the warmer months, local farmers in the region routinely report a series of ghostly lights appearing in the sky. Each time this happens, perfectly formed circles are found imprinted on the crop fields the following day.

There are those who feel that more practical explanations exist for the recurring circles. Physicist Terence Meaden of the Tornado and Storm Research Organization believes the rings are caused by "atmospheric plasma vortices," or spinning air masses that leave their mark below. Some zoologists (scientists specializing in animal studies) suggest the markings could have been made by mating deer or even large numbers of hedgehogs. Others suspect that many of the crop circles were created by hoaxers.

There have been thousands of UFO sightings in the United States, too. These include the orange lights sighted in February 1992 in Sandia, Texas, just 25 miles (40 kilometers) northwest of Corpus Christi. Tommy Kolaya, a thirty-nine-year-old businessman who had been on a family picnic, videotaped the scene. "The lights just appeared out of the

---

Circular crop indentations occur each year during the warm months in the south of England. Researchers have not been able to prove how they were formed, and UFO landing tracks make a popular theory.

sky and made some horizontal and vertical movements not like any aircraft I've ever seen before," Kolaya said. "There was no sound and no air movement either."[3] A helicopter pilot himself, Kolaya added that there was "no way the lights could have belonged to a helicopter."[4]

While there has been no shortage of UFO sightings, how many, if any, have genuinely involved aliens? Sirius, the brightest star, as well as the three brightest planets—Jupiter, Mars, and Venus—are often mistaken for alien craft traveling through space. At times, comets, meteors, and, in some instances, even the moon have been thought to be UFOs.

In a large number of cases, ball lightning, swamp gas, mirages, and distant tornadoes have been reported as orbiting alien craft. Even sunlight bouncing off flocks of birds or swarms of insects has been mistaken for spaceships. In still other instances, landing lights on airplanes, experimental military aircraft, model planes, research balloons, satellites, fireworks, and even kites have been thought to be UFOs. It is also important to consider the possibilities of

MUFON (the Mutual UFO Network) was founded in 1969. Its members are kept busy attending conferences, answering letters, and investigating sightings.

hallucination or hoax when looking into a UFO sighting. Some individuals deliberately exploit reported cases for attention, publicity, or even to develop money-making enterprises around the intriguing claims.

However, avid UFO buffs are not discouraged by the fact that numerous scientific authorities claim that most UFO sightings can be explained by other causes. These people remain hopeful that the scientists are wrong and that one day we will know more about our interplanetary guests.

Up Close With the Aliens

Numerous individuals say they have spotted UFOs in the sky. But a small yet growing number of people claim to have had more direct contact with aliens. Among them is Catherine, a twenty-two-year-old student who did not understand why she had recently experienced some unsettling feelings. Although she was unable to pinpoint the problem, it could be traced back to when she was just three years old.

During regression hypnosis (a method by which traumatic memories are recalled), she remembered awakening from a sound sleep to see a "funny-looking guy outside the window."[1]

She recalls knowing that the creature she saw wasn't human. It had "huge black eyes, a pointed chin—and his entire head . . . [was] like a teardrop inverted."[2]

Seemingly propelled by a blue light coming from behind it, the extraterrestrial, she said, passed through the window and landed at the foot of the bed. From there, Catherine claims it magnetically drew her body out from under the covers, floating her into the hall and eventually out the door.

Catherine reported that the first creature was soon joined by several others who, she assumed, came from the disk-shaped craft parked in the field next to her house. She said that after entering the craft, she saw other human children on board, playing a game with a ball and stick.

As a grown woman, Catherine, with the help of a therapist, continued to recall bits and pieces of other UFO episodes. She eventually concluded that she had had a number of encounters with alien beings. The experiences were often extremely unnerving, since Catherine came to believe that she, along with hundreds of other humans, was used as a guinea pig in the aliens' reproductive experiments.

Although it may sound incredible, Catherine's story is not as unusual as it may seem. Through regression hypnosis, thousands of individuals have begun to recall details of abductions. Those claiming to have been abducted by aliens frequently report extremely similar encounters without first having heard one another's stories. UFOlogists (people who study UFOs and related phenomena) believe these individuals tend to share a number of common experiences and reactions. Often they suffer from insomnia afterward and hesi-

Barney and Betty Hill's description of their 1966
UFO experience was used to make alien masks for
the television movie "The UFO Incident."

tate to tell other people what occurred because they do not want to be thought of as mentally unbalanced. They also usually have their own doubts to overcome.

Other commonly described aspects of most alien-human interactions are noted below:

- The majority of alien abductions are said to occur either at home or in a car late at night or in the early morning hours. The abductees are supposedly brought up to the spacecraft on a beam of blue light. While among the aliens, the abductees can pass through doors, walls, or other solid obstacles in their path.

- The extraterrestrials are frequently described as being between 3 and 4 feet (91 to 122 centimeters) tall, hairless, and grayish white in color. They are said to have oversized heads, mouths that look like slits, no ears, and huge black eyes. They do not speak out loud to either each other or the humans—all communication is telepathic.

- Supposedly, the abducted humans are medically examined by the aliens and may have sperm or egg samples taken.

- Some abductees feel they are electronically "tagged" by the extraterrestrials. This would allow the aliens to locate the humans years later, regardless of where these individuals moved.

- Numerous abductees have been returned miles from their homes or wake up in their beds with their heads where their feet should be. At times, they may be wearing their nightgowns or pajamas inside out. Once returned, some

At a MUFON convention, Betty Ann Luca poses with models of the extraterrestrial creatures she says kidnapped her. Many people have come forward with frightening stories of abduction and experimentation.

people say they find small unexplained cuts, bruises, or abrasions on their bodies in odd places. Many also claim to have experienced bleeding from their nose, ears, or rectum.

Are the majority of abduction stories genuine? Or are they merely elaborate hoaxes or perhaps the delusions of mentally ill individuals? Though in the past UFO tales were readily dismissed, recently a handful of mental health professionals have begun to take these accounts more seriously. They think that many abductees may actually be normal, healthy people traumatized by these events and in need of help.

According to psychiatrists Colin Ross of Dallas, Texas, and Shawn Joshi of Winnipeg, Canada, "Paranormal experiences [such as alien abductions] are so common in the general population that no theory of normal psychology or psychopathology [mental illness] which does not take them into account can be comprehensive."[3] These doctors believe that UFO experiences should be researched scientifically, "in the same way as anxiety, depression, or any other set of experiences," without making "any decision as to whether some, all, or none of them are objectively real."[4]

Among the most prestigious mental health professionals researching UFO abduction is John Mack, M.D., the esteemed Harvard Medical School professor of psychiatry and Pulitzer Prize winner. While Mack has never been abducted himself, he believes that a few million Americans have been. After reviewing a wide range of testimonies and interviewing numerous abductees, Mack concluded, "I saw a kind of trauma that didn't fit anything I had come across in forty years of psychiatry."[5]

Despite Mack's impressive background, his critics remain skeptical of his work with abductees. Part of the problem is that much of his data is obtained through regression hypnosis, which some regard as a questionable method. Pamela Freyd, Ph.D., executive director of the False Memory Syndrome Foundation (FMSF) noted: "Hypnosis is not a reliable tool, and memory is not a fixed thing. People can recall what they want to recall, . . . even if the events never occurred."[6]

John Mack, M.D., of the Harvard Medical School, lends credibility to the study of alien abductions. Many people feel that his research encourages the public and the scientific world to take a closer look at these incidents.

Experts in the field also stress that a hypnotist can influence his or her subject. At times, the person's responses may be swayed by what the hypnotist wants to hear. In such instances, neither the hypnotist nor the patient may realize it is happening. Some psychologists have further suggested that abductees tend to be "highly responsive to hypnosis, have intense imaginations, and find it difficult to distinguish fact from fiction."[7]

In spite of the questioning of his methods and results, Mack has continued his research. He hopes his work will eventually serve as a bridge between our world and another yet unknown to most of us.

Somewhere in Space . . .

Although a few mental health professionals are willing to consider that UFO sightings and accounts of alien abduction are real, most serious scientists doubt it. This does not mean, however, that they have ruled out the possibility of other intelligent life-forms existing within the universe.

For several decades, a number of nations have allotted staff and funding for a project known as SETI, or the Search for Extraterrestrial Intelligence.

In identifying possible locations of life, SETI scientists use large radio telescopes to electronically tune into extraterrestrial radio signals that might have been purposefully or accidentally sent to earth.

The SETI (Search for Extraterrestrial Intelligence) Institute has a sophisticated computer program that is designed to collect any signals that may come from space.

Throughout the years of electronic "eavesdropping," or listening to sounds from the universe, researchers have identified a handful of radio signals that cannot be explained. They still lack convincing evidence of other life-forms, but are encouraged by the recent discovery of material surrounding numerous stars that suggests the existence of still unknown planets. If life-sustaining planets orbit just a fraction of the billions of stars in the galaxy, countless civilizations may exist in the Milky Way.

There are various theories about why contact with aliens has not occurred. Radio astronomer John Ball at MIT believes that other life-forms in the galaxy may be too advanced to be interested in communicating with us. "They might find us interesting to study in the same way that some of our scientists spend their lifetimes studying primitive Earth life," Ball theorized. "They probably would not try to talk to us . . . for the same reason we don't try to talk to ants or bugs."[1]

Other theories have also been advanced. Frank Drake of the University of California, Santa Cruz, thinks that aliens have not come to earth because of the high costs involved. Drake reasons that no civilization would commit the necessary massive resources to a project of such doubtful gain. He feels that instead our neighbors in outer space must be pouring their time and energy into improving life on their own planets.

Dish antennae form a huge radio telescope near Socorro, New Mexico, as part of NASA's Deep Space Network for tracking and communicating with satellites and spacecraft throughout the solar system.

Respected astronomer Carl Sagan stresses
the importance of careful study in proving
that life exists on distant planets. "No one would
be happier than me if we were being visited by
extraterrestrials, but we must demand only the
most rigorous standards of evidence when
the stakes are so high," he has said.

*H. G. Wells's radio play "War of the Worlds"
sparked both terror and intrigue in all who
heard it. Are experiences with extraterrestrials
just stories, or have they really occurred?*

Still other scientists suspect that distance may be a factor in the lack of alien visits. They think the galaxy may be divided into numerous separate regions, with broad expanses of empty space between them. This would make it exceedingly difficult for intelligent life at a distant location to visit or even contact Earth.

A great deal about possible alien life is still unknown. But ongoing scientific quests may turn today's questions into tomorrow's answers.

Meanwhile, the mystery continues.

Notes

Chapter One

1. Margaret Sachs, *The UFO Encyclopedia* (New York: G.P. Putnam's Sons, 1980), p. 207.
2. William J. Broad, "Wreckage in the Desert was Odd but not Alien," *The New York Times* (September 18, 1994), p. 1.

Chapter Two

1. "The UFOs in Uncle Sam's Closet," *U.S. News & World Report* (October 23, 1989), p. 19.
2. Dennis Stacy, "Cosmic Conspiracy: Six Decades of Government UFO Cover-Ups," DMNI (April 1994), p. 38.
3. Helen Thompson, "State Wide," *Texas Monthly* (June 1992), p. 80.
4. Ibid.

Chapter Three

1. John E. Mack, M.D. *Abduction: Human Encounters With Aliens* (New York: Charles Scribner's Sons, 1994), p. 146.

2. Ibid.
3. Patrick Huyghe, "Dark Side of the Unknown," *OMNI* (September 1993), p. 36.
4. Ibid.
5. Robert S. Boynton, "Professor Mack, Phone Home," *Esquire* (March 1994), p. 48.
6. Paul McCarthy, "UFO Update: Are UFO Researchers Using Hypnosis to Manufacture Memories in Abductees?" *OMNI* (November 1994), p. 85.
7. Ibid.

Chapter Four

1. CBS News, *48 Hours*.

Glossary

astronomer—a scientist specializing in the study of stars, planets, and other bodies in space.

extraterrestrial—from somewhere other than Earth.

galaxy—a grouping of planets, stars, dust, and gas in the universe bound together by gravity; there are billions of galaxies in the universe.

guinea pig—a rodent frequently used in medical experiments, the term also applies to a human who is the object of experimentation or research.

hypnosis—a temporary state of altered consciousness sometimes used to help the subject recall repressed (forgotten) memories.

Milky Way—a galaxy consisting of the sun, moon, planets, billions of stars, and immense clouds of dust particles and gases.

psychiatrist—a medical doctor specializing in the treatment of mental and emotional disorders.

telepathy—mental communication without the use of language or gestures.

trauma—a severe emotional shock or physical wound caused by impact.

UFO (Unidentified Flying Object)—an object of unknown origin, appearing in the sky or on the ground. UFOs are often described as glowing, saucer-shaped vehicles traveling at greater speeds than that of known aircraft.

weather balloons—instrument-carrying balloons filled with hydrogen or helium sent into the upper atmosphere to measure weather conditions; such balloons, launched from weather observation stations, send information back through radio transmitters.

Further Reading

Asimov, Isaac. *Unidentified Flying Objects*. Milwaukee: G. Stevens, 1988.

Berger, Melvin. *UFOs, ETs, & Visitors From Space*. New York: Putnam, 1988.

Blumberg, Rhoda. *UFO*. New York: Franklin Watts, 1977.

Canadeo, Anne. *UFOs*. New York: Walker, 1990.

Christian, Mary Blout. *UFOs*. Mankato, Minnesota: Crestwood House, 1984.

Cohen, Daniel. *Creatures from UFOs*. New York: Dodd Mead, 1978.

———. *UFOs: The Third Wave*. New York: M. Evans, 1988.

Deem, James M. *How to Catch a Flying Saucer*. Boston: Houghton Mifflin, 1991.

Dolan, Edward F. *The Bermuda Triangle, and Other Mysteries of Nature*. New York: Bantam Books, 1981.

Kettelkamp, Larry. *Investigating UFOs*. New York: Morrow, 1971.

Knight, David C. *Those Mysterious UFOs: The Story of Unidentified Flying Objects*. New York: Parents' Magazine Press, 1983.

Mayer, Ann Margaret. *Who's Out There? UFO Encounters*. New York: Julian Messner, 1979.

Newton, Michael. *Monsters, Mysteries, and Man*. Reading, Massachusetts: Addison-Wesley, 1981.

Index